Cold Hill Pond
Michael McCarthy

Smith/Doorstop Books

Published 2007 by
Smith/Doorstop Books
The Poetry Business
The Studio
Byram Arcade
Westgate
Huddersfield HD1 1ND

Copyright © Michael McCarthy 2007
All Rights Reserved

ISBN 978-1-902382-96-8
Typeset at The Poetry Business
Printed by Swiftprint, Huddersfield

The Poetry Business gratefully acknowledges the help
of Arts Council England and Kirklees Culture & Leisure
Services

Acknowledgements
Many thanks to the editors of the following, in which
some of these poems first appeared: *London Magazine*,
The North, *Other Poetry*, *The SHOp*, *Stride*, *The Tablet*.

CONTENTS

5	Blue Jumper
7	Knitting
8	'Climbing Mount Everest' by Sir Edmund Hilary
9	Smoking
10	Eclipse
12	In the Beginning
14	Olive
15	Theologically Speaking
17	The Accident
18	Passing Out
19	Patient
20	Jasper
21	Beachcombing
22	Delayed
23	Returning
24	On Not Being a Singer
25	Is It Yourself?
26	The Town
27	Cold Hill Pond
28	A Dream of White Flowers

BLUE JUMPER

My mother knit it during the summer
specially for going to school.
She measured it against me at bed time
making sure it would fit like a shell.
It was blue as the August sky
and had double ridges down the front
that weaved in and out like fish-tails.

When I tried it on the sleeves hugged me
and the v neck was heaven.
It was fit for the High King of Ireland
or a hero like Padraig Pearse.
I felt like a hero myself.

But the teacher didn't notice,
never asked who knit it,
or gave me a sweet.

In the evening we lined up for singing:
God save Ireland said the heroes.
She didn't even notice me then.
I stood by the wall in the sunlight
stroking the ridges. It was almost
like stroking the cat's back.
She got the ruler out her drawer
came over and gave me a slap.

The stinging in my hand tingled
like the sound of the tuning fork,

or the swimming of a far off bell.
Then they began to sing: *Glory-o*
Glory-o, to the bold Fenian Men.

KNITTING

There was always knitting going on in our house.
My sisters started young.
My mother never stopped.
I helped roll the spools of wool into a ball
with my hands stretched out
like the priest when he was saying Mass.

Kitty Kelly came visiting my sisters.
She joined in. She stuck the ball of wool
inside her cardigan. They all giggled.
I said our teacher, Mrs Fitzgerald
had two apples under her jumper.
Her jumper was knitted in a shop.

They were all laughing when I said that.
They told me to go and play outside.
My mother didn't laugh when I told her
about Kitty Kelly and the ball of wool.
When I told her about Mrs Fitzgerald
and the apples she gave a smile.

Later on it got all mixed up.
Adam and Eve. The serpent. Apples.
The delicate indecencies of the moon.

'CLIMBING MOUNT EVEREST' BY SIR EDMUND HILARY

My father didn't like the Sir, it was like God Save the Queen.
And he thought climbing mountains was no trial of a man.
'There isn't much *meas* on that class of thing around here.'

I carried on reading all the same,
Tagging along behind Hilary and Tenzing.
Oxygen masks, tackle, ropes, all the gear,
Crampons, even though I didn't know what they were.

Sunday evening, somewhere between the apple tree
And the gooseberry bush, we set out from base camp.
At twenty nine thousand feet and snow-blind
I could feel the freezing inside of my skin.
I was climbing higher and higher into the thin air
When my father shouted: 'Michael. Go for the cows.'

Milking the cow in the southern stall
I imagined our final assault. The spurts of milk
On the base of the metal bucket was the sough of the wind.
The sounds growing hollow and hoarse as the bucket filled
Were our footsteps crunching the snow, our rasping for breath.

Resting below the summit, the milk almost up to the rim
The cow rolled in a great avalanche pinning me to the wall.
The bucket went flying. The milk spread like a sudden thaw,
The snow of my mountain-top melting into the straw.

Years later I read, that the first thing Hilary said was:
'We knocked the bastard off.' I liked that.

What I like now: how Tenzing knelt on the snow
On the summit of Chomolungma, the home of the gods.

SMOKING

I've never smoked, except that one time
When I found a fag in a Gold Flake box
My father thought was finished. I left it until
Sunday night when the rest of them were gone
To the dance. I listened to the top twenty first
Then snuck it inside my shirt and headed off
Down the boreen to the bottom of the hill.

There beside the well where the horses drank
I lit up and gave a pull. I watched it redden,
Then giddily blew the smoke out of my mouth.
Number one was 'Stranger on the Shore'
By Mr Acker Bilk. The excitement was
Knowing I wouldn't be found out. Next thing
A yellow hammer flew out of a furze bush.

I'm glad now that I never took it up
But I'd like to see another yellow hammer
And I wouldn't mind listening to Mr Acker Bilk.

ECLIPSE

i.m Mary Jerry Connie

Laid out there in your narrow box
your face gone small
the spitten image of your mother.

She, your father, all before you
were a fright for the pishogues
the faeries and the long dead:

– A woman washing her hands
in a bucket outside the back door.
– Voices above in the stall

doing nobody any harm.
– Lights below in the bog on a dark night
signalling from the other side!

I was never too sure about any of that
at least not since I was small.
What I am certain of

I was standing at our front door
waiting for the eclipse of the sun
when I heard the news that you were gone.

Looking up the field just after 11am
the birds silent, the light going dim,
a black heifer of Jerry Neill's turned into a man.

The neck and head grew out of
its hind quarters, it had one pair of legs!
What would the ould crowd have thought of that?

What I thought of was
the day fifty years ago,
when you came to prepare the house for a wake.

Washing the statue of the Sacred Heart,
and four year old me saying
'don't tickle him neck'

puzzled that my brother James
was lying like a statue
above in the bed.

Now you're gone wherever we go
when we leave what we have here.
The birds have stopped singing for good.

May you be among your own.
Rewarded for a kindness done.
Rarer than an eclipse of the sun.

IN THE BEGINNING

In the beginning was the Word
and the Word was the beginning
the not yet spoken spoken
the untold toldness telling

and the Word was a breath
a small spill of breath
tongue-touched into a whisper
from the beginnings of breathing

and the whisper lingered
ebbed itself over the riverbanks
out of the deepest gullies
between the swill of water and water

and the waters mirrored
the Word that was a breath
the breath that was a whisper
that became the Word in the beginning.

and the Word grew bright
in all the galaxies
in the mirror of waters
among the tall grasses

A man came, a man John.
He was not the light
but the light was in him
so that his dark breath brightened

and the stab of light
was a pillar in the valley
an arch over the holly
a shine on the wet berry

it hovered over the trees
swung from branch to branch
leaped on the hard ground
until the earth shuddered

and the Word laughed
and the Word wept
and the Word became flesh
as it was in the beginning.

OLIVE

Often, the sheets are storm tossed.
Angled elbows, knees, protrude at random. Sometimes
A turbulence of limbs breaks through the surface.
Once, her chest exposed, a withered nipple
Intimated I should look away.

Her spirit is a ship long sunk. Never a hint
Of recognition. I come here to pray with her.
Searching downward – in the blind chance
A prayer might reach her – I stand helpless.
Olive, you are no advert for old age.

Today, a nurse has been to tidy up
The bedclothes smooth and restful.
A radio plays in the background
Rod Stewart, raucous yet melodic:
Have I told you lately that I love you.

THEOLOGICALLY SPEAKING

i.m Tess Carr 1921-2003

The Church: there beside the lake
hunchbacked against the wind
since eighteen-fifty-four.

In the background
Cardinal Wiseman's cedar
growing taller every year.

Close by: the grass cut
the undergrowth cleared away
the small wooden cross now obvious.

'Who's buried here?' I ask.
'Bernadette', she says.
My eyebrows puzzle;
'The cat'.

Realising this wasn't
your average cat I hesitantly suggest,
'it's not a matter of being small-minded
or anything, but theologically speaking
Jesus didn't die for cats.
Could the grave be marked say by a shrub?'

Over a medium-sized pause
my suggestion is dismissed.

'She did enough for this Church.
Everybody loved that cat.'

Theology would have to please itself.
May Bernadette have eternal rest.

THE ACCIDENT

i.m. John A. Walsh

Autumn came early that year.
Walking in Wales – the Black Mountains –
Caught in the first snowfall. Thick flurries
Followed by bright sun. I took my shirt off.
There I am with the snowball, showing off my tan.

We stopped at Merthyr Tydfil, had steaks at the Berni Inn
Then headed back North about ten.
You always turned sentimental on those long night journeys,
College days and all that, then you'd start the Rosary.
I dropped you off near Manchester around three.

Driving over the top on the brand new M62
I take the turn off for Sowerby Bridge.
I can't tell you in what order it all broke out:

Climbing up from the gully out of the wreck
Or rolling over and over before coming to rest.
Seeing the blue lights flashing upside down,
Or the shuddering of wheels on the cattle grid.
The policeman's calm voice: 'Are you alright?
Are you alone? You don't have to say anything
But anything you do say…' and so on.

It's all clear now, thirty two years later:
Picking up the golf clubs strewn along the slip road,
Whispers of cold air on my neck.
Pulling my jacket through the back window
The sound of glass on the road when I give it a shake.

PASSING OUT

As I relate how
the sudden loss of balance
unbalanced me, how the nausea spread
until my face could feel itself turning
from colourless to turquoise white

how I hovered this side of passing out
having no say in anything until
the doctor came, and how
lying in the ambulance
it seemed to head in the wrong direction

I remember that after I'd let go of worrying
it occurred to me: if this is how we take our leave
it is less distressing than some things
I can think of, say unrequited love
or missing a train.

PATIENT

Knowing how I hate hospitals, I try to
distract myself with people whose plight
is worse than mine. William Trevor's
Beyond the Pale and Other Stories.

It doesn't work. Noticing the elderly couple
opposite, I next peruse the colour scheme,
the lighting, the glass-topped double doors.
Through them, down a long corridor I see
security guards with guard dog approaching.
I can't actually see the dog, just the dog chain.
A security man is holding it with both hands.

Coming through the doors into full view,
they're not security guards, and it's not a dog,
and the man in the green surgical gown
is not a medic. He is handcuffed to the chain
which is handcuffed to a guard. They lead him
up the stairs and out of sight. Voyeurs
caught in the act we look away.

Someone out of prison tells me later
his dread of hospital appointments.
The most humiliating part: how people
out of pity turned their heads away.

JASPER

      Lying there on the green couch
I drift into the equilibrium of sleep.
I'm running through a tunnel of evergreens
towards a temple with a shine on its stone steps
their sharp edges transient as rivers
– it could be Venice – and then climbing
into a bell tower that becomes a hedge
beyond which a train approaches
steady as the beat of an old song
and from a grassy mound your voice
clear as daybreak reaches across
the frozen lake to the glacier.
We're the age we always were.
I awake to the residue, the dream
already silk scarf, snow-melt.

BEACHCOMBING

after George Mackay Brown

On day one a pair of dolphins appear. They swim parallel
                                        to the shore.
We watch each other then they are gone. I see them no more.

On day two I search the shingles and find a flat blue stone.
I skim it into the shimmer of waves. I lose it in the sun.

On day three I sail out of Boston on board the Whaler Catalpa.
Our mission: the rescue of Fenian convicts off Freemantle.

On the fourth day a fine-figured blonde woman walks my way.
I see the skin of her neck is shrivelled, her face half eaten away.

On the fifth day a hermit crab crawls out of his shell.
In time he'll grow another. I'll keep the original.

On day six at dawn a black woman walks out of the sea.
Says she is Queen Esther; she'll heal me under the medicine tree.

On day seven I read about scalping in Texas in 1849.
A white horse rides by with pink fetlocks, blood-orange mane.

On the eight day a waiter in Mickey Mouse gear says
                                        the food is good.
Five hundred percent better than yesterday. Guaranteed.

Sundown, day nine, the incessant sound of an African drum.
Prevent-us-from-error. Prevent-us-from-error. From-error. Amen.

DELAYED

Breathless as if running up steps
or in a tizz getting ready for Mass

chalice – paten – hosts – water & wine
trying to keep the altar servers to a whisper

while all the time it was only because
I missed my turn off at Ainley Top

and had to drive all the way up the moors
past the place where the motorway splits

because the man who played the tin whistle
wouldn't let them through his house in 1967

to the exit at Saddleworth and the cattle grid
where I got turned over in 1971

then all the way back along the reservoir
seventeen miles to the very same spot

and trying to make up for lost time
I took what I thought was a short cut

past the Infirmary, the Children's Library,
the man walking his dog, the street littered

with the smell of last night's fish and chips
to these traffic lights stuck forever on red.

RETURNING

On the way back I was ablaze.
I was the white light that hits
coming up out of the pothole.
I was a dazzle to myself.

I was at last the fossil-filled
framework of myself.
Because I said what I said,
because I blurted it out.

And for the first time on this earth
I was standing in my own shoes,
on the other ground of myself.
I was mine. Entirely mine.

Pulling into the service area
I looked out over the lake
and let myself spread
as far as I could.

I rang you and said I was
sorry, then sat at the lakeside
breathing in everything
for which I was not sorry.

ON NOT BEING A SINGER

      I've always wanted to be a singer,
To let my voice follow the song as far as it could,
Glide out over the crowd. I can do it all right in my head.
Last night in the mirror inside the sacristy door I was
Ray Charles. 'I can't stop loving you'. It was perfect.
Except for the voice, and the fact that I wasn't black.

Willie Nelson. Maybe I could do that, or Pavarotti,
The way he belted it out before the World Cup.
But not like the old tramp on O'Connell Street that night
Before the All Ireland: his arms outstretched, head thrown back,
His slurred eyes oblivious to the crowds as they streamed past,
And no sound whatsoever coming out of his mouth.

My father was a fine singer. His father before him
Taught all his children to sing. As a boy he had wanted to
Go off and sing like Caruso, as John Mc Cormack did later on.
He stayed on the farm, and raised thoroughbred horses instead.
My uncles and aunts could all sing. My father's songs were
'Hard times come again no more', and 'The ship
                        that never returned'.

IS IT YOURSELF?

After the race I go to the unsaddling enclosure.
The horse ran well. The owner's had an each-way bet.
He's satisfied enough. After the jockeys have weighed in
I'm invited to the owner/trainer bar. I listen as they
talk the talk. He'll come on for this. Good to soft
is what he likes. The ground last time out was heavy.
Beyond us, in the large wall mirror: the trainer,
the owner and the owner's friend, and beyond them
out of the corner of my eye an older man, smart jacket,
white hair, handsome, standing just behind me.
Discreetly I turn my head. There's no one there.
In the mirror I look again, this time full on.
He's there all right. Dark jacket. White hair.

THE TOWN

'Brazen,' they said.
'Brazen as brass monkeys.'
The way the pair of them paraded
up and down the town, without an ounce
of shame on them, their skirts barely covering
their knees; head-lamps you never saw the like of.
'Them two will have no bother getting husbands,
if they last that long.' They both married young.

Today I saw one of them, I'm almost certain,
meandering down Main Street. Slow moving,
ponderous, pensionable.

While up in North Street, Minihane's Public House
is as it always was. The narrow doorway, and inside
my father drinking porter with old men, as they talk
about the troubles. Kilmichael, Crossbarry, how they
beat the Black and Tans. The back yard down to the river
is overgrown, the stables derelict. But the tide is in,
and if I close my eyes I'll smell the horse manure,
hear the harness bells.

COLD HILL POND

There are things it's not necessary to know.
The depth of the pond for instance. Who cares?
Its depth is upwards. The mirror it makes
Is what matters, and what that mirrors:

The movement of clouds. The wide canopy of trees
Before the leaves fall. The double breasted swan
Still as sadness, her domed wings rippled
Contemplative, the tips joined in prayer.

This pond is not for swimming. It's for seeing
What is in the sky and what is not in the sky:

The bales of straw, stacked and square
Like towers of a Taj Mahal,
The peleton of Canada geese flying south,
Away from the blank cold, away from
The minus of things, to wherever
The swan imagines. I'm glad

It sits beside this twist of road
Each time I take the corner, too fast
For the fact of silence, for the depth of its
Imagining, for the slow heartbeat of the sun.

A DREAM OF WHITE FLOWERS

Someone is putting flowers round the bed
Where I'm sleeping. Someone is saying
How much I'm welcome.

Awakening, though not yet awake
Hospitality seeps into me. Penetrates
My shield of disbelief. Of late

I've been alien to myself.
So-what-ing my accomplishments.
I have lived in that cold climate.

And now visited by friends
And now this dream! I am
Knit back into my history.

The bed is large, luxuriant.
The duvet cover warm and dark.
The flowers – there are lots of them – all white.